# TIGER SHARKS

# The Amazing World of Sharks

# The Amazing World of Sharks

# TIGER SHARKS

By Elizabeth Roseborough

MC MASON CREST

Mason Crest
450 Parkway Drive, Suite D
Broomall, Pennsylvania 19008
(866) MCP-BOOK (toll-free)
www.masoncrest.com

First printing
9 8 7 6 5 4 3 2 1
Printed in the USA

ISBN (hardback) 978-1-4222-4131-8
ISBN (series) 978-1-4222-4121-9
ISBN (ebook) 978-1-4222-7680-8

Library of Congress Cataloging-in-Publication Data

Names: Roseborough, Elizabeth, author.
Title: Tiger sharks / Elizabeth Roseborough.
Description: Broomall, Pennsylvania: Mason Crest, [2019] | Series: The amazing world of sharks | Includes bibliographical references and index.
Identifiers: LCCN 2018013895 (print) | LCCN 2018018841 (ebook) | ISBN 9781422276808 (eBook) | ISBN 9781422241318 (hardback) | ISBN 9781422241219 (series)
Subjects: LCSH: Tiger shark--Juvenile literature.
Classification: LCC QL638.95.C3 (ebook) | LCC QL638.95.C3 R684 2019 (print) | DDC 597.3/4--dc23
LC record available at https://lccn.loc.gov/2018013895

Developed and Produced by National Highlights Inc.
Editor: Keri De Deo
Interior and cover design: Priceless Digital Media
Production: Michelle Luke

# CONTENTS

## KEY ICONS TO LOOK FOR:

**Words to Understand:** These words with their easy-to-understand definitions will increase the reader's understanding of the text while building vocabulary skills.

**Sidebars:** This boxed material within the main text allows readers to build knowledge, gain insights, explore possibilities, and broaden their perspectives by weaving together additional information to provide realistic and holistic perspectives.

**Educational Videos:** Readers can view videos by scanning our QR codes, providing them with additional educational content to supplement the text. Examples include news coverage, moments in history, speeches, iconic sports moments, and much more!

**Text-Dependent Questions:** These questions send the reader back to the text for more careful attention to the evidence presented there.

**Research Projects:** Readers are pointed toward areas of further inquiry connected to each chapter. Suggestions are provided for projects that encourage deeper research and analysis.

**Series Glossary of Key Terms:** This back-of-the book glossary contains terminology used throughout this series. Words found here increase the reader's ability to read and comprehend higher-level books and articles in this field.

# FUN FACTS...
# GETTING TO KNOW THEM

## TIGER SHARK
Named for the vertical striped markings along its body, but they fade with age.

## MAKO SHARK
Known as the race car of sharks for its fast swimming speed!

## BULL SHARK
Named for its stocky shape, broad, flat snout, and aggressive, unpredictable behavior!

## RAYS
Rays and sharks belong to the same family. A ray is basically a flattened shark.

**GREAT WHITE SHARK**
With jaws this fierce, they don't call it "Great" for nothing!

**BLUE SHARK**
Known by their distinct blue and white coloring, their large eyes, and long snout.

**HAMMERHEAD SHARK**
Yes, those are eyes mounted on the side of its head, giving it 360-degree vision!

**THRESHER SHARK**
This clever shark uses its unique long tail fin to stun and catch prey!

**WORDS TO UNDERSTAND:**

near threatened: Any species of animal that is likely to become vulnerable or endangered in the near future.
predator: An animal that naturally preys on other animals.
scavenger: An animal that feeds on dead animals, especially a carnivore that eats dead animals in addition to hunting live prey.

## CHAPTER 1

# INTRODUCING TIGER SHARKS

It's a part of human nature to be scared of animals that can harm us. From spiders to snakes to sharks, it's normal to experience a fast heartbeat and rapid breathing at the mere sight of these creatures! Over hundreds of thousands of years, our natural warning systems have adapted to alert us to nature's many dangers, and this instinct to stay away from animals that can harm us may feel scary, but it's actually important for keeping us safe. The more we learn about sharks, the less scary they become. Shark attacks are not as frequent as the news and movies make them out to be, and sharks (especially tiger sharks) are actually important to ocean ecosystems.

Tiger sharks are scary, but they're essential to our oceans' ecosystems.

Believe it or not, great white sharks are not the scariest sharks in the ocean.

When we think of the scariest, most dangerous shark in the ocean, many of us immediately think of the great white shark. Our minds conjure up an image of a huge, gaping mouth, a large gray body marked with battle scars, and razor-sharp teeth, and we start sweating at the mere thought of sharing the water with such a creature. While that idea is correct in many ways—great whites indeed are the most common perpetrators of shark attacks on humans—the lesser-known tiger shark, also known as the man-eater shark or the sea tiger, is not far behind when it comes to violence and ferocity.

Found in both coastal and deepwater areas throughout the world, tiger sharks are named for the dark, vertical stripes that are often seen on juvenile tiger sharks (these stripes nearly disappear near adulthood), allowing for excellent camouflage. Unlike a great white, a tiger shark is unlikely to swim away after it bites a human (or an animal)—these giant, vicious fish tend to stick around until the job is finished, which is a part of

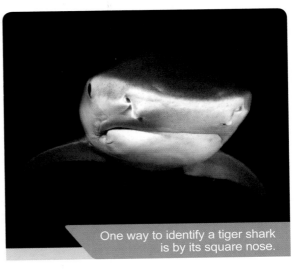

One way to identify a tiger shark is by its square nose.

why these sharks have such a scary reputation. Tiger sharks do not seem to care about the taste of what they eat, and once they get a bite of something, they keep eating until it's gone. When surfers see the telltale square nose and bluish-green fin of a tiger shark coming their way, they know they need to get to the shore as fast as they can. In areas where tiger sharks are common, local residents know how important it is to watch for signs that they are nearby.

*Listen to this surfer tell the story of being attacked by a tiger shark off the coast of Hawaii.*

The coast of Hawaii is an area well known to be a hotbed of tiger shark activity. In the video on the previous page, the surfer foolishly ignored the warning signs before getting into the water. Amazingly, he lived to tell the tale. Watch the video again and pay special attention to the warning signs the surfer mentions.

Tiger sharks have been around since dinosaur times, and studies suggest that they have changed, grown, and adapted to their environment just like other animals who have stood the test of time (specifically turtles, snakes,

Tiger sharks have inhabited the oceans long before humans arrived.

fish, and birds). It's likely tiger sharks will continue to successfully evolve, even with the global climate change the world is currently experiencing.

Tiger sharks adapt well to their environment, easily changing their diet and adjusting to different water temperatures. The one thing that tiger sharks cannot keep themselves safe from is a human hunter.

Scientists are doing all they can to save tiger sharks.

More and more governments are making laws to keep the tiger shark safe, but unfortunately, some hunters continue to kill these giant sharks, as their body parts are worth a lot of money in some areas of the world. Conservation efforts so far have been very successful, but there is still much work to be done to ensure that tiger sharks do not eventually become extinct.

Tiger sharks tend to be both curious and aggressive when they spot humans, a combination that can often prove deadly. Tiger sharks are much more likely to attack humans who are on the surface of the water (such as swimmers and surfers) than humans who are exploring the ocean floor (such as scuba

Tiger sharks prefer to live along the coast.

divers). Tiger sharks tend to hang out in dark, murky, shallow coastal waters, making it easy for them to hide from their next snack before sprinting through the water to make their kill.

While tiger sharks do attack, even when unprovoked, they do not go out specifically looking for humans. Tiger sharks do not often go out looking for any one type of food. They're opportunistic eaters, meaning that if they're hungry, they'll take a bite of anything that comes their way. They're like the dogs of the ocean world, eating whatever, whenever. Scientists find everything from turtle shells to license plates to old tires in the stomachs of tiger sharks!

As you'll soon learn, tiger sharks have incredibly unique serrated teeth that allow them to bite without considering whether or not something is edible—unlike many ocean animals. Their teeth and jaws are unlikely to be harmed by chomping into a non-food object. Marine biologists call tiger sharks the "dustbins of the seas," as they are quick to clean up trash and debris that fall to the ocean floor. These giants fall into both the **predator** and the **scavenger** category of the ocean food chain, sometimes even eating younger tiger sharks.

Tiger shark teeth are designed to rip and pull apart prey.

While they spend plenty of time scavenging for the leftovers of other predators, tiger sharks are excellent hunters. While stalking their prey, they sink to the bottom of the ocean, usually concealed by murky waters or sea grass, waiting for the perfect moment to sprint towards the surface and

Tiger sharks like to eat albatross, but won't turn down other delicacies.

## SHARK MYTH: WHEN TIGER SHARKS ATTACK HUMANS, THEY'RE JUST CONFUSED.

While many shark attacks on humans are simply a case of mistaken identity, scientists believe that this is simply not true for tiger shark attacks. Tiger sharks have unusually keen senses (they're known for their fantastic low-light vision and sense of smell), and know exactly what they're attacking as they're sneaking up on their prey. Unlike great white sharks, it's unlikely that a tiger shark will take a bite of something and choose not to finish their meal. While scientists cannot be completely sure of what's going on inside a tiger shark's brain, it appears that the vast majority of the time, tiger shark attacks are intentional—either because they are trying to protect themselves or because they want something to eat. Tiger sharks will also bite humans if they feel that the human poses a threat, either to their physical safety or to the success of their hunt. Tiger sharks will indeed feast on people when given the opportunity—as well as dogs, horses, and tires. While many animals are simply confused when they attack humans, tiger sharks do not fall into this category!

Although tiger sharks adapt to their environment, their numbers are dwindling.

attack their unsuspecting prey. Tiger sharks are committed to traveling long distances to get to one of their favorite foods: albatross, a large ocean bird that tends to live on the Hawaiian coast. Migration is one of the rare times that tiger sharks can be found swimming in the open ocean. They usually prefer to stay close to land (and food).

Growing up to 25 ft. (7.62 m) in length and weighing up to 1900 lbs. (about 862 kg), it's hard to imagine that anyone or anything could threaten a tiger shark, but sadly, they are currently classified as a **near threatened** species. Hunters go after tiger sharks heavily because the shark's fins, liver, and skin are loaded with vitamin A. These nutrient-rich organs are then processed into expensive vitamin oils. Tiger sharks take a long time to reproduce, and they are being hunted faster than they are being born. In areas with a lot of tourists, some people kill sharks and then attempt to sell their teeth as vacation souvenirs. It's not a good idea to buy shark teeth on vacation. Usually, the teeth are fake, but even if they are real, it's likely that a shark had to be killed in order to get the teeth.

## IS SHARK HUNTING LEGAL?

Shark hunting laws are different in each part of the world. In most parts of the United States and Europe, shark hunting is illegal. In some areas of Asia, shark hunting is permitted. No matter what part of the world you're in, shark hunting negatively affects the ocean's ecosystem. Sadly, many fishermen continue to hunt sharks even though it is illegal. It's difficult for police to know what fishermen are doing when they are away from the shore.

There have also been incidents of communities hunting tiger sharks after a person has been attacked, either out of fear or out of revenge. While killing tiger sharks may feel like the right thing to do after a person has been injured or killed, this does little to stop other tiger sharks from coming into the area. The best thing that can be done to keep people safe is to learn about sharks and their habits, and create a warning system to let people know when sharks are in the local area. Scientists are working hard to learn as much as they can about the migration and hunting habits of tiger sharks so that they can help people stay safe by giving them as much information as possible.

While tiger sharks can be scary, they are fascinating creatures that should be treated with respect. It's important that we learn more about these amazing animals and their role in ocean ecosystems.

 **TEXT-DEPENDENT QUESTIONS:**

1. How did tiger sharks get their name?

2. When it comes to attacking humans, tiger sharks are different from great white sharks. How?

3. Tiger sharks are a near threatened species. What does this mean?

 **RESEARCH PROJECT:**

Tiger sharks are often called the "dustbins of the seas" due to the odd variety of items that have been found in their stomachs. What happens to these items once they are in the tiger shark's stomach?

**WORDS TO UNDERSTAND:**

**atoll:** A ring of islands made up of coral reefs.
**brackish:** A mixture of fresh river water and salty seawater, found where rivers meet oceans.
**estuary:** The area in which a river or stream meets an ocean or bay.

## CHAPTER 2

# THE TIGER SHARK'S POPULATION AND HABITAT

It's hard to pin down exactly where the tiger shark makes its home. Tiger sharks have a tendency to follow food, and they move frequently. While most sharks have an area of the ocean that they call home, tiger sharks do not have a set habitat since they are constantly moving. So far, scientists have been unable to find a pattern to help make their frequent movement more predictable. There are a few things that we do know about their preferences, however. Tiger sharks typically seem to enjoy warm waters, such as those in the Caribbean and the western Pacific (especially near Fiji and Australia), but can be found in a variety of areas, including colder

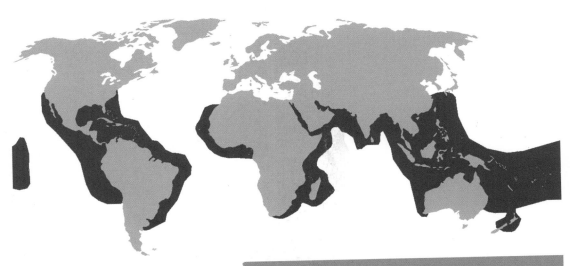

The tiger shark's estimated habitat is vast.

waters. Tiger sharks can also be found in the coastal waters of China, India, Africa, and Japan. Although tiger sharks are known for preferring these warmer waters, they have also been known to make their homes as far north as Cape Cod on the northeastern coast of the United States. They are willing to go wherever their favorite foods are, and they are known to travel long distances to hunt animals that appeal to them. Lurking anywhere from just below the surface to depths of up to a half-mile, tiger sharks are constantly searching for their next meal!

There are three areas in the world in which tiger sharks are most regularly spotted—Shark Bay off the coast of Australia, Shark Bay north of the Bahamas, and off the coast of Hawaii. While tiger sharks are seen in these three places with more regularity than anywhere else in the world, this does not mean that these are the only places that tiger sharks make their home. It's likely that they are seen here due to the fact that food is plentiful along the shoreline, making the sharks more likely to be seen by humans than when they're in the middle of the ocean. Tiger sharks have very little fear of humans, which means it's important that people in these areas are hyperaware when sharks are in the water, in order to prevent an attack. These areas are perfect for scientists to learn more about tiger sharks.

Tiger sharks are often located in Shark Bay in Western Australia.

## WHY DON'T WE KNOW MORE ABOUT THE TIGER SHARK'S HABITAT?

Tiger sharks tend to go where the food is, and they're unlikely to stay in one place for long. Scientists are beginning to track tiger sharks, but in order to track them, they must first find them so that they can give them a tracking device. Many scientists do this off the coast of Hawaii.

## NEAR THE COAST

Tiger sharks usually prefer to spend most of their time in areas that are very close to land in order to find their prey of choice (turtles, birds, sea snakes). This is a part of why so many humans are scared of tiger sharks—these predators regularly lurk in areas that humans typically use to surf and swim. Most people who live in the coastal areas that tiger sharks frequent have seen a tiger shark at some point in their lifetimes. There are warning signs—certain seasons, certain smells—that let local people know when a tiger shark is likely to be nearby, and it's important to pay attention to these signs and alert others when they occur.

*Watch a large number of sharks swimming in Shark Bay World Heritage Area.*

Many tiger sharks do well in **brackish** waters, and some have even been known to swim up **estuaries**, as well as through **atolls**, harbors, and streams, often swimming and hunting near human activity. While tiger sharks are able to swim in very deep water (more than half a mile deep, or .8 km), they also have been found in areas as shallow as 8 ft. (about 2.5 m), often hiding in sea grass, searching for their next meal. It's scary to think

When surfing in shark waters, it's important to pay attention to shark warnings.

about, but tiger sharks often hide very close to where the water meets the land, waiting for birds or turtles to come close enough for them to eat. The sharks' dark stripes allow them to easily camouflage themselves as they swim through the grass, making their presence nearly undetectable to their prey. Their ability to hide and willingness to swim so close to the shore makes a human encounter very likely.

Tiger sharks linger in sea grass looking for prey.

Many sharks prefer to stay in saltwater, and scientists are not sure why tiger sharks seem to be happy to swim in brackish waters. Most likely, tiger sharks are willing to push through water that might not be their favorite in order to satisfy their appetites. These giant fish will do pretty much anything for a tasty treat, including swimming up to forty miles (or more) per day. Tiger sharks do not appear to have a pattern that they follow when it comes to feeding. It seems that they swim around until they find a good hunting spot, and when the food runs out, they move to a new location.

As long as there's food, a tiger shark will stay in one location.

## TRACKING

Most sharks are predictable. They go one place in the morning, one place at night, one place to hunt, one place to rest—but tiger sharks are different, as they are difficult animals to track. They do not stay in one place for long, and they're always looking for new hunting opportunities. Some tiger sharks do show up in the same place day after day, but some will show up in one place, disappear, and then reappear years later. There does not seem to be much reason to when they disappear and reappear. Scientists are just beginning to understand where tiger sharks live, hunt, and socialize with one another.

It's believed that this unpredictability is part of what makes tiger sharks such successful hunters. Animals that tend to fall prey to tiger sharks do not know how to avoid them, as they can never be sure where tiger sharks are lurking. This is another reason that it's difficult for scientists to track

Although loners, tiger sharks do at times swim with other sharks.

Studying tiger sharks helps keep them safe.

tiger sharks. Usually, sharks follow their prey, but since tiger sharks do not have a very discerning palate, they are harder to track based on their eating habits. Most scientists believe that there is some type of pattern to a tiger shark's movements; they just do not have enough information to figure out exactly what that pattern is yet.

Marine biologists are working hard every day to learn more about the tiger shark's movements. This is important for two reasons. First, learning more about where the tiger shark goes (and when it goes there) is essential for keeping people safe, since tiger sharks are so likely to attack humans if they encounter each other in the water. Secondly, it's important to know where tiger sharks are so that conservation efforts can be made to keep these animals safe from fishermen who try to harm or kill them.

### HOW DO MARINE BIOLOGISTS TAG SHARKS?

Tagging a shark is not an easy task. The first step is catching the shark in a large net. Scientists then use a pulley system to bring the shark on board the boat, where they are able to weigh the shark, take photographs, and check that the shark has not already been tagged. Most tags are attached to the shark's dorsal fin. This does cause a moment of pain for the shark, but most scientists agree that the pain is worth the protection the tag allows them to provide for the shark. Tagging a shark can be a dangerous process—many scientists have dealt with injuries caused by shark bites after the shark is on the boat. By learning more about sharks through tagging, scientists are able to do more to ensure that sharks continue to thrive.

There are two main types of tags that scientists use to track tiger sharks: satellite tags and acoustic tags. Satellite tags are attached to the shark's dorsal (top) fin, and send a signal to a receiver every time the dorsal fin breaks the surface of the water. This type of tracking allows scientists to learn about when and where sharks travel, what other sharks they interact with, and how often they come to the surface of the water. Satellite tracking technology is getting more sophisticated every day. Scientists are now able to use this technology to pinpoint almost exactly a shark's travels through the ocean.

Acoustic trackers work a little bit differently. A tag is still attached to the shark; however, instead of sending a signal to a satellite, it sends an audible ping at set intervals (anywhere from every few hours to every few days). Receivers are set up underwater to record these noises. Each time the noise is recorded, scientists know that a shark is in the area of the receiver. Acoustic trackers are great for letting scientists know how often sharks frequent certain areas, but they are not particularly helpful for learning more about a shark's migrations or behavioral patterns.

*Watch this video to learn more about how scientists are studying sharks with tracking devices.*

## MIGRATION

Scientists know that tiger sharks tend to migrate to warm tropical and subtropical locations when their usual hunting waters get cold, but no one is quite sure why, as some tiger sharks seem to prefer more temperate waters. Some scientists hypothesize that the sharks are following their prey—mainly birds—as they migrate south for the winter. Tiger sharks prefer to spend their time in shallow coastal waters, but they do quite well in deep ocean water as well.

Tiger sharks tend to visit the same feeding areas repeatedly, but so far, scientists have not been able to figure out whether or not they're following a pattern, or simply following the food. Tiger sharks tend to visit the same feeding areas every two weeks to ten months. Amazingly, tiger sharks seem to have a keen sense of direction—they remember where they've been and how to return.

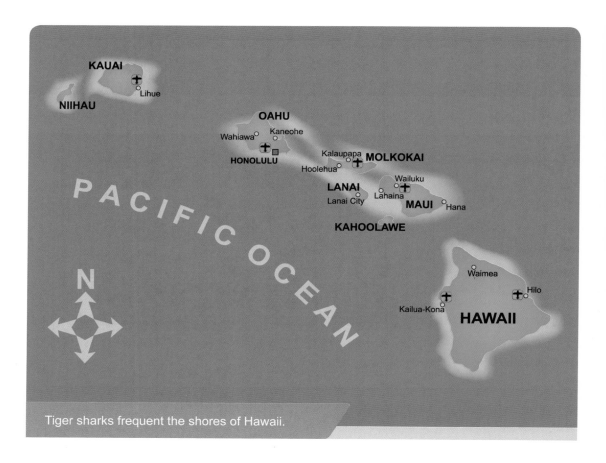

Tiger sharks frequent the shores of Hawaii.

Tiger sharks are most likely to be seen in Hawaii in the fall. Surfers in Hawaii call this time Sharktober! Many scientists believe that the tiger shark's fall migration has to do with their mating patterns. Female tiger sharks are likely to be pregnant in the fall (with up to eighty baby sharks at one time), and therefore, are extremely hungry. Knowing that their favorite food— albatross—are plentiful in Hawaii may be enough to convince these female sharks to make the long journey to the islands. It's also possible that most sharks simply prefer the warm waters that Hawaii has to offer, and make the trip there when their usual home begins to experience the chill of autumn. In recent years, shark attacks in Hawaii have increased, and scientists are not sure why this is happening. This may be due to an increased number of people swimming in the ocean around the islands during the fall.

Tiger sharks often eat sea turtles.

## HOW MANY ARE LEFT?

Over the past twenty years, the number of tiger sharks caught in the wild has declined. While it's good that fishermen are catching fewer tiger sharks, this may also be a sign that their population is going down. As apex predators, it's important for the balance of the ocean's ecosystem that tiger sharks remain plentiful. If the population of tiger sharks continues to decrease, the animals that the tiger shark normally preys upon will increase, which can cause a negative chain reaction of issues for ocean animals. For example, tiger sharks regularly eat sea turtles. Sea turtles eat a lot of the sea grass that grows on the ocean floor. If there are not enough tiger sharks to hunt sea turtles, the turtles are likely to eat all of the grass on the ocean floor, not leaving enough food for other ocean creatures. While it's sad to think of a tiger shark eating a sea turtle, it's important that the ocean's ecosystem stays in balance.

People often hunt sharks for their fins, which kills the shark.

As a near threatened species, it's important that protective measures are taken to protect tiger sharks from becoming endangered or extinct. Many countries have put laws in place that make it illegal to hunt tiger sharks, but sadly, some fishermen have found ways around this. In Southeast Asia, it's common practice for hunters to capture tiger sharks, cut off their fins, and return them to the water. The fishermen know that they can get a lot of money when they sell a shark fin (up to $100 per fin). Sadly, the shark is unable to survive without its fin, as it is no longer fast enough to be able to hunt. Eventually, sharks without fins starve to death. Some fishermen also hunt tiger sharks for their skin, which can be sold as expensive leather.

Not all tiger shark kills are intentional. Often, fishermen are attempting to catch other types of sharks, and end up killing tiger sharks along the way. It's important that all sharks be protected, as hunting for one type of shark while leaving others alone is impossible. Tiger sharks are often harmed or killed in nets that are meant for catching tuna fish.

At times, the fear of tiger sharks has even led the government to encourage people to kill sharks, even when the sharks have not attacked. In the 1950s, the Hawaiian government offered rewards to fishermen who caught and killed tiger sharks, in an effort to keep swimmers and surfers safe from attack. While it is always scary to be in the water and know that sharks could be nearby, it's important to remember that the likelihood of being attacked by a shark, even in a place like Hawaii, is one in five million. Shark killing programs do not actually work to keep people safe, as sharks do not tend to stay in one area long enough for a program like this to have a significant effect on lowering the likelihood of shark attacks. Today, the people of Hawaii respect tiger sharks and no longer try to harm them. Some Hawaiian legends state that tiger sharks have mystical powers, often connected to their extremely powerful sense of vision.

This Polynesian shark pattern is sometimes used for tattoos.

## HOW COASTAL DEVELOPMENT HURTS OCEAN LIFE

Coastal development is another reason that the tiger shark population is declining in some areas. When cities build houses or businesses along the coastline, it can destroy the habitat of the animals that live there. This can hurt tiger sharks when they are there to hunt, or remove their food source, making it difficult for them to live a healthy life.

Tiger shark population growth is very dependent on the laws that governments make to protect them. For example, the Bahamas are considered a shark sanctuary. This means it's illegal to kill or harm sharks in the waters surrounding the Bahamas. Tiger sharks are regularly seen around the islands. When sharks are protected, their numbers grow. In 2012, Florida enacted a law that makes it illegal to kill tiger sharks, but until then, shark hunting was legal. We must do our part to protect these giant fish and keep our oceans healthy.

Increased human population affects tiger shark numbers.

## TIGER SHARKS AND GLOBAL WARMING

With global temperatures on the rise, it's clear that some animal populations will increase while others decrease. The tiger shark population is likely to rise due to a few factors. First, tiger sharks prefer warm water. Increasing ocean temperatures will not negatively affect their ability to breed or hunt. Secondly, tiger sharks will eat basically anything. While they prefer certain animals, such as sea turtles and albatross, they have no issue eating something different if their favorite cuisine is in short supply. Lastly, a female tiger shark's ability to have many babies at one time (up to eighty pups in each pregnancy, with pregnancies occurring approximately every three years) is likely to cause resurgence in the tiger shark's population over time.

Baby tiger sharks are called pups.

 **TEXT-DEPENDENT QUESTIONS:**

1. What's the difference between an acoustic tracker and a satellite tracker?

2. What's one probable reason that tiger sharks travel to Hawaii each fall?

3. Name three places in the world where tiger sharks are likely to be found.

 **RESEARCH PROJECT:**

Many scientists believe that the tiger shark population will increase as ocean temperatures continue to rise. Do scientists hold this same prediction for other species of sharks?

**WORDS TO UNDERSTAND:**

countershading: A type of camouflage in which an animal's body changes from a light color to a dark color, allowing the animal to blend in with a variety of surroundings.

omnivore: An animal that eats both plants and other animals.

terrestrial animals: Animals that spend most of their time on dry land.

# CHAPTER 3

## THE TIGER SHARK'S DIET, BEHAVIOR, AND BIOLOGY

### DIET

The tiger shark is one of the least demanding eaters of all ocean creatures. As **omnivores**, tiger sharks will eat plants or animals—pretty much anything that comes their way. While many sharks eat a variety of foods, the tiger shark has the most diverse diet of all sharks. Tiger sharks will eat bony fish, jellyfish, lobsters, crabs, sea snakes, sea birds, seals, turtles, stingrays, manta rays, and other sharks. Dolphins used to be a favorite food of tiger sharks, but dolphins have learned to avoid areas with lots of sharks.

Dolphins have learned to avoid shark-infested waters.

Tiger sharks will also eat **terrestrial animals**, such as dogs and horses, if they are able to get close enough to them. A tiger shark is not able to leave the water and attack on land, but if a terrestrial animal ventures into the ocean and a tiger shark is waiting for its prey in the murky water below, the shark will quickly attack. Terrestrial animals tend to be easy prey for tiger sharks, as land animals are not used to being aware of the water below. Tiger sharks can quickly launch a surprise attack on an unsuspecting land animal.

Tiger sharks have been known to attack unsuspecting land animals.

Tiger sharks also eat human trash that floats out to sea, and this is just one of the many reasons it's so important to keep our oceans clean. While sharks can easily bite and swallow garbage, the trash then sits in their stomachs for years and causes damage to their digestive systems. An amazing array of trash has been found in the stomachs of tiger sharks. Items found include undetonated ammunition for bombs, paint cans, even a full suit of armor!

The best way to protect tiger sharks is to keep our oceans free of trash.

## HUNTING

Tiger sharks are expert hunters, and their tiger-like stripes allow them to camouflage themselves better than most ocean predators. When hunting, tiger sharks sink to the bottom of the ocean, making themselves nearly invisible to their prey. Most of the time, tiger sharks are slow, quiet swimmers, but when it's time to hunt, everything changes. Using their powerful fins, tiger sharks sprint from the bottom of the ocean towards the surface, catching their prey by surprise. Tiger sharks are in the hunt for the long haul—they are unlikely to take a bite of their prey and then move on to something else.

Tiger sharks have a light-colored belly that also works as camouflage. When they are swimming at the top of the ocean, potential prey at the bottom of the ocean have trouble seeing the sharks because they blend in with the lighter color of the ocean's surface created by the sun. This **countershading** means that no matter where tiger sharks are in the ocean, they are hidden from their prey. Usually, tiger sharks prefer to hunt at night. The darkness makes it even easier for them to blend in with the bottom of the ocean, hiding from their prey, but they certainly are not limited to only hunting at night.

Tiger sharks evolved to blend in with the ocean.

Tiger sharks are known for being aggressive. When they hunt, they are there to get the job done. Tiger sharks are curious, but unlike the great white shark, they will not take a bite out of something (or someone) just to see what the taste is like—when they're hunting, their prey is very likely to be destroyed.

Scientists observe tiger sharks eating a variety of animals, both ocean dwelling and terrestrial. They have even been observed eating man-made garbage, such as tires, from the ocean's floor.

*Watch this video to see a tiger shark attack!*

## BEHAVIOR

The tiger shark is aggressive during hunting, and this tendency does not turn off when interacting with other sharks. Tiger sharks are known to attack one another if they feel provoked. For the most part, tiger sharks are solitary animals that prefer to hunt and travel alone. It's rare that scientists observe tiger sharks traveling in schools.

Tiger sharks are solitary.

As an apex predator, it's rare that other animals will attack tiger sharks, but it does happen from time to time. Killer whales (also known as orca whales) have been known to attack tiger sharks. Great white sharks have been known to attack tiger shark pups. At times, tiger sharks will even attack and eat the pups of other tiger sharks.

## BIOLOGY

While not all tiger sharks grow to this size, females can grow up to 25 ft. (7.62 m) in length and weigh up to 1900 lbs. (862 kg). Tiger sharks are one of the few species in nature in which females tend to be larger than males. While we usually think of sharks as being light gray in color, the tiger shark's skin can actually range from light green to blue on the tops of their bodies, and their bellies are the typical gray and white color of most other sharks. Their stripes are always darker than the rest of their body, and usually fade to some degree as the tiger shark becomes an adult. The stripes never completely go away, but they are much lighter in fully mature tiger sharks.

A tiger shark's head is fairly flat and wedge shaped. This shape allows the shark to make quick turns, essential for a successful hunt. Like great white sharks, tiger sharks also have electrosensitivity, meaning that they have small pits on their noses that allow them to sense electric fields. This means that they know when other animals are nearby even if they are so far away that they are unable to be smelled or seen.

Tiger sharks are designed for stealth.

Tiger sharks (and other sharks) also have an organ called the lateral line that runs down their backs, from their head to their tail. The lateral line is a sensitive narrow tube that is filled with fluid. This allows them to detect tiny vibrations in the water, which signals that there is an animal nearby. Most ocean animals have a lateral line, but not all have the level of sensitivity that a tiger shark does. Inside the lateral line are cells that are similar to hairs. The tiniest change in the vibration of the water causes these cells to move, and signal to a shark's brain that there has been a change in the water. Over time, tiger sharks learn that different types of vibrations mean different animals are nearby, and they can use this knowledge to decide whether or not it's time to hunt. These tiny vibrations can also help keep tiger sharks safe, alerting them if the rare potential predator is nearby. When deciding whether or not to eat an object or animal, tiger sharks have been known to purposely bump into the object, getting a good read with their lateral line. Many scientists believe that a combination of the shark's excellent sense of smell, electrosensitivity, and use of their lateral line are a large part of what makes them excellent hunters, even when it's very dark.

Tiger shark noses are very sensitive.

**SHARK MYTH: SHARKS CAN DETECT A SINGLE DROP OF BLOOD!**

While sharks do have an excellent sense of smell, it is not possible for them to detect a single drop of blood in vast ocean waters. Sharks do have a different way of smelling, however. Their nostrils are located on the underside of their snout. Part of the reason a shark's nose works better than a human's nose is because they are used solely for smelling—not for breathing. Sharks use their noses to detect predators and prey, and female sharks even use their noses to smell pheromones—chemicals given off by potential mates. Even though sharks cannot detect a single drop of blood, it's never a good idea to get in the ocean if you have an open cut.

The tiger shark's skeleton is made up of cartilage (a tough material that takes the place of bone) that is reinforced with minerals to keep the shark's body strong. Tiger sharks have small scales that are embedded in their skin.

Tiger sharks have excellent vision. Their eyes work differently than a human's eyes. Behind a tiger shark's retina, there is a reflective layer that allows light to be trapped. This allows the tiger shark to see extremely well in low-light conditions, such as when they are hunting at night in murky waters or tall sea grass. This is important, as sharks must constantly swim. Unlike fish that are filled with bones, sharks are actually heavier than water and will sink if they stop to rest. A tiger shark's liver is filled with oil that helps to keep it afloat. Oil has a lower density than water, meaning that oil-filled objects have an easier time floating to the top of the water than more dense objects. The shark's oil-filled liver helps absorb some of the effort needed to keep swimming. While swimming, it's essential that tiger sharks leave their mouths open. This ensures that sea water, rich with oxygen, constantly flows over the shark's gills, allowing the shark to breathe.

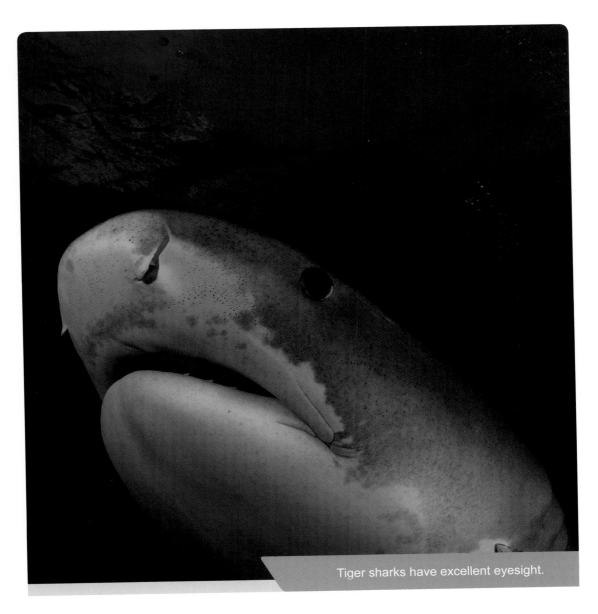

Tiger sharks have excellent eyesight.

While tiger sharks generally swim slowly, their unusually long fins allow them to sprint through the water when it's time to attack their prey. They usually use small, repeated movements of their fins to propel them through the water before they attack. These small movements allow them to sneak up on their prey without alerting other animals to their presence.

Dorsal fin

Dorsal fin

Caudal fin

Anal fin

Pelvic fins

Pectoral fins

The tiger shark's fins help it hunt and swim.

Tiger sharks have two dorsal fins on the topside of their bodies. These dorsal fins are in-line with the lateral line. Dorsal fins are what we think of when we picture a shark attack, but sharks have other important fins as well. The caudal fin is the shark's tail, and allows the shark to control its speed, which is especially important when it's hunting its prey. The anal and pelvic fins are on the underside of the shark, and they allow it to control its movements with great precision. The pectoral fins are also on the underside of the shark, but near the front of its body. These fins work a bit like arms—they allow the shark to push its body through the water, helping it to speed up or slow down in conjunction with the caudal fin.

The tiger shark has very unusual teeth, and these strange teeth are a part of what allows them to be such aggressive and successful predators. Their teeth are serrated, just like the cutting edge of a saw. The points of their teeth face sideways, instead of up and down. This unique mouth design allows tiger sharks to rip into flesh, muscle, bone—even metal objects—without causing harm to their jaws. The serrated edges of the teeth grind together when the shark closes its jaw, allowing the shark to rip into its prey without having to invest a large amount of effort. It's typical that a tiger shark will lose teeth while hunting for its prey, but this is not a problem, as its teeth constantly regenerate over the course of its lifetime. Unlike humans, most sharks have an endless supply of teeth. Just like we regrow our hair and fingernails, a shark's body is constantly growing new teeth.

Tiger shark teeth are very distinctive.

Female tiger sharks become pregnant approximately once every three years. Her babies (up to eighty of them!) grow in baseball-sized eggs inside her body. Before the babies are born, they hatch out of the eggs, and are born live into the water. Baby tiger sharks, also known as pups, are very flexible and covered in dark stripes. Most tiger shark pups are about 30 in. (76 cm) long at birth, and covered in very dark stripes that will begin to fade as they get older. After tiger shark pups are born, they are on their own and receive absolutely no care from their parents. While the pups are certainly smaller than the adults, they are otherwise fully developed. They look like miniature versions of their parents, and immediately start swimming around and looking for food, without help from their mothers.

Tiger sharks can birth up to eighty pups.

Because scientists are still learning so much about tiger sharks, it's hard to say exactly how long they live. They are estimated to have a lifespan of at least fifteen years, but many scientists believe that their actual lifespan might be thirty to forty years. As tagging technology continues to improve, more information will be learned about tiger sharks' lifespans.

## TEXT-DEPENDENT QUESTIONS:

1. Tiger sharks will eat anything. Why is it dangerous for them to eat garbage?

2. How does the lateral line help tiger sharks hunt?

3. How many babies do female tiger sharks have at one time?

## RESEARCH PROJECT:

Tiger sharks have a special organ called the ampulla of Lorenzini. This is the organ that allows sharks to detect electromagnetic fields. Research how this organ works and why it is so essential to a shark's survival.

**WORDS TO UNDERSTAND:**

**cage dive:** A type of shark dive in which the diver is enclosed in a steel cage. This allows the diver to view the shark without being in danger of a shark attack.

**coral:** Hard, colorful calcium deposits that bind together to create a reef and places for fish to live.

**free dive:** A type of shark dive in which the diver freely swims with sharks, without being separated by a cage.

# CHAPTER 4

## ENCOUNTERING A TIGER SHARK

While many people are afraid of tiger sharks, there are also some who are curious and want to learn more about them (and you may very well be one of these people). Swimming with tiger sharks can be dangerous, but it's something that many divers do regularly! It's possible to dive with tiger sharks with or without a cage. When **cage diving**, divers are completely enclosed in a steel box, with bars close enough together that a shark is not able to enter the cage. This offers an up close and personal view of the shark without the danger of free swimming.

This crew lowers a metal shark cage for divers into Ganis Bay off the coast of South Africa. Researchers continue to study tiger sharks because little is known about them.

Diving without a cage is risky, but exhilarating. During a **free dive**, divers go down to the ocean floor, as being at eye level with sharks helps the shark see the diver as an equal, rather than as prey. Many divers who regularly swim with tiger sharks speak of the sharks' unique personalities—some are playful, some are serious, and some are affectionate. Tiger sharks will swim freely with divers, chasing after fish and showing off. Whichever route you'd like to take to encounter a tiger shark—cage diving or cage-free swimming—there are two main places in the world where you're likely to get to experience these amazing creatures.

Tiger sharks allow divers to get very close.

Regardless of the style of dive, they all begin the same way. The tour guide will chum the waters by throwing bloody pieces of fish overboard to attract sharks to the dive area. Usually, sharks show up within minutes to get a snack. Before the dive begins, most tour guides will feed the sharks some fish, such as mackerel. This helps to distract the sharks from the divers entering the ocean, and ensures that they aren't too hungry when the dive begins. While sharks are rarely aggressive in diving situations, it's important to do your dive with an experienced guide who will know the personalities of the sharks in the area and be able to keep you safe.

It's important to remember that if you see a shark when not part of a dive, you must get out of the water. A shark dive is not something that you can safely attempt on your own, no matter how much you have learned about sharks.

## TIGER BEACH, BAHAMAS

Tiger Beach is not actually a beach at all. It's an area of the ocean approximately 25 mi. (40 km) north of the Bahamas that is known for its shallow waters and frequent tiger shark sightings. The clear-as-glass water is 25 - 40 ft. (7.62 - 12.19 m) deep, and conditions are ideal for divers to experience tiger sharks up close and personal. Most dives in Tiger Beach are cage free, and typically, this is a feat left to more experienced divers (it's not something a first-time diver should try). The sharks in this area are used to divers, and often come around to get the snacks that divers bring for them.

Tiger Beach in the Bahamas is a popular place for divers to see tiger sharks.

It's important to note that while it's unlikely to get attacked by a shark during a professionally supervised cage-free dive, it does happen. In 2014, there was a likely fatal shark attack during a supervised dive in Tiger Beach. A tiger shark attacked a diver, dragged him away, and the diver was never seen again. While diving with sharks is exciting and can be fun, it's important to remember that the sharks are wild animals, and their behavior will never be completely predictable. Shark swimming can be fun, but it's vital to remember to respect wild animals, no matter how calm the situation may seem.

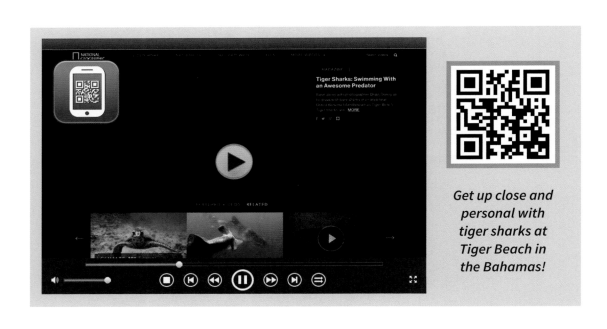

*Get up close and personal with tiger sharks at Tiger Beach in the Bahamas!*

Don't let the name fool you—this beach is not actually a beach at all. This small area of shallow water, filled with **coral**, is located about 25 mi. (40 km) away from Grand Bahama Island. The conditions here make this an ideal place to see tiger sharks in action. The water is crystal clear—divers strap on weight, sink to the bottom, and get to see tiger sharks in their natural habitat. Most tiger sharks in Tiger Beach are used to interacting with divers and do not seem to view them as prey.

## WHAT SHOULD I DO IF A TIGER SHARK ATTACKS ME?

First of all, it's important to note that it's incredibly rare to get attacked by any kind of shark. To put the odds into perspective, in 2015, there were thirty-four human fatalities from dog attacks, and only five from shark attacks. Prevention is the most effective method of avoiding a shark attack.

Although it might seem cool and adventurous to enter into the water when you see a shark fin, it's a terrible idea. You should immediately move away from the water and alert a lifeguard if you think you see a shark. Staying out of the water early in the morning and late at night can help keep you safe from sharks, as you're more likely to be able to see them in broad daylight.

If, however, you do find yourself in a situation in which you need to fend off a shark, there are a few tips to help you get away. First, scream for help. This will alert those around you to your situation and will likely startle the shark. Second, fight back. Sharks are not used to prey fighting back, and if the shark feels threatened, it may back away. Third, when you do break away from the shark's grasp, do not turn your back on the shark. Swim towards the shore in a way that allows you to keep an eye on the shark, so that it is not able to sneak up on you. The fact that the shark sees you watching it may be enough to get it to swim away.

## OAHU, HAWAII

Tiger sharks seem to be everywhere in Hawaii! There are many companies that offer cage diving off the coast of Oahu. Remember, cage diving is a little bit safer than free diving, but still will give you the chance to get up close and personal with a tiger shark. The best time of year to go shark diving in Hawaii is in the fall, specifically, in October. In the fall, tiger sharks show up in large schools (which is unusual, as these animals typically travel alone).

It's rare that tiger sharks will be aggressive towards divers in cages. They tend to swim along with the boat, enjoying the snacks provided by the tour guide, giving divers a close view, and then swim away when the food is gone.

Cage diving in Hawaii is very popular.

## ONLINE SHARK TRACKING

If you aren't able to dive with sharks but still want to learn more about them, many websites give you the ability to track sharks online. You will be able to follow sharks in real time and see where they are migrating. This is an awesome way to learn more about the behavior patterns of sharks if you are unable to actually see them in the flesh. See the internet resources section in the back of this book for some ideas on where to get started with online shark tracking.

## TIGER SHARKS IN CAPTIVITY

Whether or not sharks should be kept in captivity at all is a controversial topic. Sharks tend to have shortened lifespans when they are kept in aquariums, most likely due to the fact that they are more stressed when they are removed from their natural environment. However, there are a few aquariums in the United States that do currently have tiger sharks as a part of their exhibits.

The National Aquarium in Baltimore, Maryland has tiger sharks on display for visitors to view. This aquarium also offers an event called "Sleepover with the Sharks" in which you can sleep over at the museum! The Waikiki Aquarium on Waikiki Island in Hawaii also has tiger sharks available for public view.

It's rare to see sharks in captivity. The Shark Pool of Coral World Underwater Observatory aquarium in Eilat, Israel is the biggest shark pool in the Middle East.

## TEXT-DEPENDENT QUESTIONS:

1. How is cage diving different from free diving?

2. When is the best time to go shark diving in Hawaii?

3. If a tiger shark attacks you, what should you do?

## RESEARCH PROJECT:

Research more ways to encounter tiger sharks. Based on your research, decide if you think human encounters with tiger sharks help conservation efforts (by making people more aware of sharks) or hurt conservation efforts (by making people more afraid of sharks).

# SERIES GLOSSARY OF KEY TERMS

**Apparatus:** A device or a collection of tools that are used for a specific purpose. A diving apparatus helps you breathe under water.

**Barbaric:** Something that is considered unrefined or uncivilized. The idea of killing sharks just for their fins can be seen as barbaric.

**Buoyant:** Having the ability to float. Not all sharks are buoyant. They need to swim to stay afloat.

**Camouflage:** To conceal or hide something. Sharks' coloring often helps camouflage them from their prey.

**Chum:** A collection of fish guts and fish remains thrown into the ocean to attract sharks. Divers will often use chum to help attract sharks.

**Conservation:** The act of preserving or keeping things safe. Conservation is important in keeping sharks and oceans safe from humans.

**Decline:** To slope down or to decrease in number. Shark populations are on the decline due to human activity.

**Delicacy:** Something, particularly something to eat, that is very special and rare. Shark fin soup is seen as a delicacy in some Asian countries, but it causes a decline in shark populations.

**Expedition:** A type of adventure that involves travel for a specific purpose. Traveling to a location specifically to see sharks would be considered an expedition.

**Ferocious:** Describes something that is mean, fierce, or extreme. Sharks often look ferocious because of their teeth and the way they attack their prey.

**Finning:** The act of cutting off the top (dorsal) fin of a shark specifically to sell for meat. Sharks cannot swim without all of their fins, so finning leads to a shark's death.

**Frequent:** To go somewhere often. Sharks tend to frequent places where there are lots of fish.

**Ft.:** An abbreviation for feet or foot, which is a unit of measurement. It is equal to 12 inches or about .3 meters.

**Indigenous:** Native to a place or region.

**Intimidate:** To scare or cause fear. Sharks can intimidate other fish and humans because of their fierce teeth.

**Invincible:** Unable to be beaten or killed. Sharks seem to be invincible, but some species are endangered.

**KPH:** An abbreviation for kilometers per hour, which is a metric unit of measurement for speed. One kilometer is equal to approximately .62 miles.

**M:** An abbreviation for meters, which is a metric unit of measurement for distance. One meter is equal to approximately 3.28 feet.

**Mi.:** An abbreviation for miles, which is a unit of measurement for distance. One mile is equal to approximately 1.61 kilometers.

**Migrate:** To move from one place to another. Sharks often migrate from cool to warm water for several different reasons.

**MPH:** An abbreviation for miles per hour, which is a unit of measurement for speed. One mile is equal to approximately 1.61 kilometers.

**Phenomenon:** Something that is unusual or amazing. Seeing sharks in the wild can be quite a phenomenon.

**Prey:** Animals that are hunted for food—either by humans or other animals. It can also mean the act of hunting.

**Reputable:** Something that is considered to be good or to have a good reputation. When diving with sharks, it is important to find a reputable company that has been in business for a long time.

**Staple:** Something that is important in a diet. Vegetables are staples in our diet, and fish is a staple in sharks' diets.

**Strategy:** A plan or method for achieving a goal. Different shark species have different hunting strategies.

**Temperate:** Something that is not too extreme such as water temperature. Temperate waters are not too cold or too hot.

**Tentacles:** Long arms on an animal that are used to move or sense objects. Octopi have tentacles that help them catch food.

**Vulnerable:** Something that is easily attacked. We don't think of sharks as being vulnerable, but they are when they're being hunted by humans.

# INDEX

# FURTHER READING:

**Compagno**, Leonard; Dando, Marc; & Fowler, Sarah. *Sharks of the World* (Princeton Field Guides). Princeton: Princeton University Press, 2005.

**Discovery Channel**. *Sharkopedia*. Silver Spring: Discovery/ Time, 2013.

**Klimley**, Peter. *The Secret Life of Sharks*. New York City: Simon & Schuster, 2007.

**Parker**, Steve. *The Encyclopedia of Sharks*. Ontario: Firefly Books, 2005.

**Skomal**, Greg. *The Shark Handbook: Second Edition: The Essential Guide for Understanding the Sharks of the World*. Kennebunkport: Cider Mill Press, 2016.

# INTERNET RESOURCES:

**http://www.pacioos.hawaii.edu/projects/sharks/**
Check out this map to follow shark travels in real time! This site will show you where sharks are around the Hawaiian Islands and allow you to track their movements over time.

**http://cnso.nova.edu**
The Halmos College of Natural Sciences and Oceanography provides shark videos and shark activity maps.

**http://cnso.nova.edu/sharktracking**
The Guy Harvey Research Institute (GHRI) Shark Tracking partners with the Halmos College of Natural Sciences and Oceanography in tracking and recording shark activity. The GHRI dedicates its resources to the preservation of marine life, including sharks.

**http://saveourseas.com**
The Save Our Seas Foundation focuses their efforts specifically on saving sharks and rays. Their website includes shark facts, a newsletter, and details about how to help save sharks and rays.

**https://www.discovery.com/tv-shows/shark-week/**
The Discovery Channel's shark week offers information on all types of sharks. Their site includes information on shark habitats, hunting habits, and conservation efforts.

# AT A GLANCE

Source: www.iucnredlist.org

**SWIM DEPTH**

- 200 ft.
- 400 ft.
- 600 ft.
- 800 ft.
- 1,000 ft.
- 1,200 ft.
- 1,400 ft.
- 1,600 ft.
- 1,800 ft.

**Hammerhead Sharks**
Length: 20 ft. (6.1 m)
Swim Depth: 262 ft. (80 m)
Lifespan: 20+ years

**Bull Sharks**
Length: 11.1 ft. (3.4 m)
Swim Depth: 492 ft. (150 m)
Lifespan: 18+ years

**Rays**
Length: 8.2 ft. (2.5 m)
Swim Depth: 656 ft. (200 m)
Lifespan: 30 years

**Great White Sharks**
Length: 19.6 ft. (6 m)
Swim Depth: 820 ft. (250 m)
Lifespan: 30 years

**Blue Sharks**
Length: 12.5 ft. (3.8 m)
Swim Depth: 1,148 ft. (350 m)
Lifespan: 20 years

**Tiger Sharks**
Length: 11.5 ft. (3.5 m)
Swim Depth: 1148 ft. (350 m)
Lifespan: 50 years

**Thresher Sharks**
Length: 18.7 ft. (5.7 m)
Swim Depth: 1200 ft. (366 m)
Lifespan: 50 years

**Mako Sharks**
Length: 13.1 ft. (4 m)
Swim Depth: 1,640 ft. (500 m)
Lifespan: 32 years

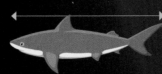

# PHOTO CREDITS

# EDUCATIONAL VIDEO LINKS

## Chapter 1
Listen to this surfer tell the story of being attacked by a tiger shark off the coast of Hawaii: http://x-qr.net/1ENZ

## Chapter 2
Learn more about how scientists are studying sharks with tracking devices: http://x-qr.net/1Gwc

## Chapter 3
Watch this video to see a tiger shark attack! http://x-qr.net/1Cts

## Chapter 4
Get up close and personal with tiger sharks at Tiger Beach in the Bahamas! http://x-qr.net/1HWN

# AUTHOR'S BIOGRAPHY

Elizabeth Roseborough is a former college, high school, and middle school biology instructor. When not visiting her favorite Caribbean islands, Elizabeth spends her time with her husband, son, and their fur babies, Titan and Stella, at their home in Dayton, Ohio.